# Abundance

## The Secret Principles of using The Law of Attraction to Manifest Wealth, Love, Happiness and Anything You Can Imagine

By Tim Reid

Copyright 2014 by Tim Reid.

Published by Make Profits Easy LLC

Profitsdaily123@aol.com

facebook.com/MakeProfitsEasy

# Table of Contents

Introduction..................................................................6
   Get off the spinning wheel. ...........................7
   The power is within us. ................................. 8
Chapter 1 – What is the Law of Attraction? ...... 11
   The Law of Attraction ...................................13
   How this all relates to our daily lives. ............ 16
Chapter 2 – The Power of Energy...................... 21
   The power of positive.................................... 23
   How we can use energy to improve our lives. 25
Chapter 3 – Transforming Energy..................... 32
   Know what you want..................................... 32
Chapter 4 – Understanding *You* ........................41
   What you want. ............................................. 43
   What you don't want..................................... 46
   How to reach your true inner desires.............47
   Why knowing all of this is important. ........... 50
Chapter 5 – Attract the Things You Want .........52
   Wealth ............................................................54
   Happiness.......................................................56
   Love ................................................................57
   Career ............................................................ 58

Success ................................................................. 59

Health ................................................................... 60

Abundance ........................................................... 61

Chapter 6 – Learning to Ask for the Things You Want ...................................................................... 63

Law of attraction begins by opening yourself up to what you want. ........................................ 64

Asking is important. ......................................... 68

Open yourself up to allow these things into your life. ............................................................. 70

Chapter 7 – Real Stories of People Who Used the Laws of Attraction ............................................... 76

Conclusion ........................................................... 84

# Introduction

Do you know what the laws of attraction are? They are all around us. Every single one of us. Anything you want in life –as long as it's physically possible- can be attained when you approach getting it the right way.

Too many people stand around and wait for life to hand them what they want, rather than going out there and getting it.

I'm not talking about the physical effort that it takes to become successful. There are plenty of people out there actively engaged in the famous 'rat race' and some are getting ahead while the majority of them are simply 'spinning their wheels' and getting no closer to their dreams than when they started.

Just stop and take a look around you at this very moment. Check out the neighbors across the street. Think about friends you had in high school. Consider all of the people you have connected with on social media. The vast majority of them may *seem* like they are doing great, that they have everything they could ever have wanted, but that's simply not true.

We live in a society where image (what others think of us) seems to be more important than what you actually have and, more important than that, the dreams that you've *made* come true.

## Get off the spinning wheel.

You want the best that life has to offer. You deserve it. While you might have been spinning your wheels all this time, working 40, 50, or maybe even 80 hours a week trying to get as much money as you could so that you can afford the nice clothes, the new car, and even a nice home, you're still not fulfilled.

You probably still feel empty.

The worst part is that you're probably trying to figure out why. *Why am I so unfulfilled even though I have 'stuff?'*

It's because you aren't becoming *wealthy*. You might not have found true *love*. You're not *happy*.

Most of us are raised to believe that earning money is the key to everything. It's not.

The Law of Attraction is.

This is not about getting the girl or the guy you want (although you will find that to be possible once you learn about the Law of Attraction). It's about something much deeper than that.

## The power is within us.

Every single one of us possesses the power to attract *all* of the things we want, as long as we develop the right attitude and the right *energy*.

We can change our entire life with just a change in attitude. That's right. Nothing is out of your grasp when you approach things with the right attitude and mindset.

Don't let anyone ever tell you that just because you didn't go to college or because you're too short or fat or whatever that you can't do or have what you want. There are numerous stories of people who should *never* have done the things they did, but because they had the right attitude, they made it so.

If you truly want to change your life and obtain or achieve anything you can imagine, then you need to step back from the way things have always been done in your life, the way you've always thought about things, and approach them from a completely new perspective. When you do, you'll be amazed by what's possible.

The Law of Attraction was written from the dawn of time. It's not something that mankind created. It's real and it's right there, waiting for you to discover it.

But why don't more people know about it?

Because, frankly, too many people envy those who get what they want and they simply don't believe in the Law of Attraction so they will do everything they can to make sure no one they know pursues it. They simply can't figure it out so, to them, it must not be real.

It is. And you can discover it.

And get everything you ever wanted.

# Chapter 1 – What is the Law of Attraction?

In our life, we have been programmed from early on that 'attraction' is pretty much all about getting the girl (or guy) you like to like you back. It's been made to have an almost strictly sexual connotation.

That's a tragedy, actually, because while men and women are ultimately attracted to one another, that's just one small component of attraction. It doesn't really have anything to do with the Law of Attraction.

The attraction that you feel to another person is innate, instinctual. The Law of Attraction is something that exists within and throughout the universe. It's bigger than any one person. In fact, it's bigger than *all* of the people who are and have ever lived.

Think about that for a moment.

All of the people who have ever lived on this wonderful planet we call Earth, the billions upon billions through tens of thousands of years, collectively, are still not more significant than the Law of Attraction.

Why?

Because it's the basic foundation upon which *everything* in the universe was built. Without the Law of Attraction, stars and planets would not have been formed. The 'Big Bang' would never have occurred. Any noble gases that had been floating around in an endless space would have continued floating, never concentrating into a miniscule mass and then exploding into the universe we know today.

Without attraction, galaxies would not have formed. The earth would never have existed, and you wouldn't be here.

It's that important, that fundamental, and that powerful. So what, exactly, is it?

## The Law of Attraction

The Law of Attraction basically states that every good or bad thing that happens to an individual is the result of what you wanted.

That may sound quite harsh for someone who feels as though nothing is going right in his or her life, who may feel as though they are losing control. But it's true.

Don't misunderstand this. The Law of Attraction is *not* stating that you *deserve* anything bad that's happened to you any more than someone else *deserves* the good things that come their way.

It's stating simply that what you have brought to you, or what has come to you, has done so based solely on you and what you have been *attracting* to you.


*The conundrum.*

This opens up a wide range of ideas. Have you ever looked at someone else, noticed that he or she seemed to always be smiling and happy and that nothing but good things would come their way?

Did you ever think to yourself, 'He's such a jerk, he's so mean to some people ... why does he *always* get what he wants?' Most of us have at one time or another.

Head down to your local bar on a Friday or Saturday night and you'll see at least one person who seems to always get friends, has money, and seems relaxed and easy going. Yet he's a complete jerk who didn't finish high school and you just want to know what his secret is.

His secret is simple: he understands the laws of attraction and uses them to get what he wants. He might not actively understand those laws or that they exist, but he's using them all the same.

In truth, we are born with the knowledge of these laws embedded in our DNA. However, as we grow up and are taught by our parents, teachers, friends, and society as a whole, we're programmed to think and act *contrary* to those laws.

They are pushed away from us. That's pretty sad when you think about it.

So now, when you're having a bad day and nothing seems to go right for you and no matter how unfair it seems (or how hard you try to change it, even though you can't), here's the harsh reality: *you attracted that to you.*

This will probably get at least a few of you spitting mad at me for saying that, and that's okay. You need to go through those emotions because when you begin to understand the laws of attraction better, you'll realize that it's true.

Even though you don't really want bad things happening to you, your mindset and the energy that you portray is actually drawing them to you.

## How this all relates to our daily lives.

Consider that time when you woke up late for school or work. Maybe you were out late the night before and you turned the alarm off while still half asleep, or you forgot to set the alarm.

You jump out of bed in a panic. *You're setting the tone for your day right there.*

The thoughts that are jumping through your mind are this:

- Oh man, I can't be late *again*!
- Why didn't I set a second alarm?
- I bet the traffic is going to *suck*.
- I don't have time to eat breakfast ... I'll just grab a coffee on the way.
- This is bad. This is *really* not good.

Take a good look at those thoughts. Are *any* of them good? The answer is no.

Not one of those statements or thoughts have anything positive interlaced within them. I **can't** be late again. Why **didn't** I set a second alarm? I bet the traffic is going to **suck**. I **don't** have time ... This is **bad** ...

As you can see, even these seemingly innocent observations about what actually happened are drawing negative energy into your world. You're anticipating that the traffic is going to be tough. So you end up hitting every red light (or so it seems).

When you're in a hurry, it *always* seems as though you hit all of the traffic, red lights, and slow drivers on the road, right? Why is that? Why is it that you always seem to be screwed when you're late?

Is it because only during those moments are those lights turning red? Or is it because your mindset is such that you're *expecting* that to happen?

Now you finally get close to your job. You're already late so you figure a couple of extra minutes to stop and grab a coffee is no big deal. You step into the Starbucks or other café and the line seems like it's out the door and never going to move. You check your watch repeatedly, thinking '*Why me?*'

Then you finally get to work and your boss is railing on you about being late ... *again.* You bear the brunt of his anger because you need the job. You *need* this job. It's not that you want it, but you can't get anything else. (That's another negative mindset). You have rent to pay, a car payment to make, and you need food. So you *need* the job.

So why are you constantly late? That's an easy answer. It's one of two: you either don't respect your boss or coworkers or you just don't really like this job or care about it.

And thus you are stuck in a vicious cycle of negativity through which you will continue to attract bad things to you.

Now, let's change things just a bit.

You go out after work that day. You head to a local pub and sit by the bar nursing a $10 drink, asking yourself why you just spent so much for a mixed beverage when an attractive person asks if they can sit down next to you.

You smile politely and introduce yourself. You begin small talk and before long, you realize you have a lot in common with this person. You exchange phone numbers and end up going on a date.

You're on Cloud 9 and can't believe it. You go home feeling great and wake up the next morning feeling the same way. Suddenly the traffic isn't as bad, your boss is nice to you, and things begin looking up. Your job doesn't suck as much as you thought it did the day before.

Your day is now completely different than it was just one day prior. But what changed?

Your *attitude*. Without even realizing it, you began attracting *positive* things to you and positive things began to happen.

Does that mean whenever you're positive *only* positive things will happen? Of course not, but unless you begin to attract them to you, they will remain elusive and you'll continue to wonder why other people seem to have all of the success in life while you continue to scrape out an existence that doesn't seem fair in the least.

The laws of attraction exist for *anyone*. You simply have to understand how they work so that you can put them to work in your life and manifest all the abundance that you could possibly want.

# Chapter 2 – The Power of Energy

If you can remember some tidbits from your high school science classes, then you probably recall something about energy.

There are essentially two forms of energy in the universe: positive and negative.

Energy is constant in the universe as well. That means that all of the energy that exists right now is all that ever existed and all that will ever exist.

*Wait, what about power plants or cars? What about those things that create electricity?*

Yes, power plants create electricity. Solar panels do, too. But they aren't creating *energy*. They are merely transferring energy from one source to another. There's active and passive energy. Fossil fuels that are sitting under the surface of the earth are passive sources of energy. When that oil is extracted, processed, and then turned into gasoline, it's still passive. Once it's poured into your car's gas tank then moved through the line to the engine's combustion chamber and then the spark plug fires it, *then* it becomes active. That passive energy was transferred into the power to move your car.

Now that energy was converted into exhaust and released into the atmosphere as $CO_2$, or carbon dioxide where it will then eventually be used by plants or trees or something else.

Energy is constant and there are only two forms.

Look at a battery. There will be a plus (+) sign as well as a minus (-) sign on it. Those symbols represent positive (+) and negative (-) polarity. Both are required in order to make the battery power the device you're using. The polarity is *not* the same as positive and negative energy, though. Yet, to some degree it is.

If you take two magnets, one positive and one negative *polarity* (which is not the same as energy), what happens? They attract one another, right? And two same polarity magnets will repel, right?

Energy is just the opposite. Positive energy attracts positive energy and negative energy attracts negative energy. Energy is constant, remember, so there is going to be the same amount of positive energy in the universe next year as there is today and as there was 4 billion years ago.

Someone is going to attract positive energy which means someone else is going to attract negative energy. It's just the basic fundamentals of the universe. Do you want to be the one who attracts negative energy all the time?

You've already seen what it does to your life and your mindset. It's no fun, is it?

**The power of positive.**

You might have heard about the 'power of positive thinking.' It's a concept that was developed by life coaches and other professionals to help their clients begin to develop a different mindset and draw out the positive aspects of their life.

It's really a very simple concept: begin to think positively, even when things are going bad, and those negative issues will filter away and positive things will begin happen to and for you.

In other words, when you *think* positive, you *become* positive. Add the laws of attraction and we can say: *think* positive and you *become* positive ***energy***. That positive energy that you become will attract more positive energy and thus good things in life.

We're going to get into transforming energy in the next chapter, but before we do, you need to understand something very important about energy and its basic laws.

When someone talks about transforming energy, they are misrepresenting what actually happens. Since energy is constant, you can't really change its polarity. You *can*, however, change the kind of energy that you *attract* to yourself.

If you have been experiencing nothing but negative things in your life recently, you're attracting them to you. So in order to change your life, you will need to transform yourself and thus the basic groundwork upon which energy is drawn to you. You won't be transforming the energy around you but rather attracting something different to you.

I know this all sounds rather confusing at the moment, but trust me, it will all come together in time, before the end of this book and you'll know exactly how to change your life completely.

## How we can use energy to improve our lives.

I want you to think back on your life for a moment. I want you to go to a quiet place where no one will be able to interrupt you. I want you to turn off your phone and make sure that you can get some quality, uninterrupted time by yourself.

Now, once you're there, I want you to look back on your life, as far back as you can go. Take a notebook or simple sheet of paper and begin to write down all of the times when you can remember being happy. I mean truly happy. These would be moments when you didn't think that anything could be better, that you just didn't want the days to end.

It might have been a summer when you were a young teenager hanging out with your best friends. It could have been a family vacation where everyone was getting along and you were laughing all the time.

Write these memories down.

Now, I want you to now think back and recall periods of your life when things never seemed to go right, when you couldn't wait for the day, week, or season to end. No matter what you did, nothing seemed to go right.

Again, write these memories down.

Now, think about each of these various memories and try to recall what was happening to you before they occurred? If you can accurately remember those events leading up to those periods of time in your life, you'll notice a pattern.

Before the wonderful memories, things were going fairly well. They might not have been 'great' by your adult definition, but to your younger self, they were pretty good just before those wonderful memories, right?

And just before those bad times, things were sort of coming apart at the seams, correct? They might be considered minor issues to you now, but when you were younger, they could have been major problems. Bad grades, you got punished because you lied to your parents, or something else.

Leading up to those profoundly bad memories were some bad days or events. They seemed to build up to that horrible moment in your life.

Notice a pattern? You should. If you don't, then you need to think deeper and find the accurate memories, but *they are there*. Make no mistake about it ... right before the wheels seem to come off of your life were a series of negative events.

Don't misunderstand death, serious illness, or accidents to someone you care about having anything to do with you or the energy surrounding you. We're talking about aspects of your life that *you* could control. Losing a loved one suddenly is *not* related to the laws of attraction.

In every positive *and* negative period of our lives, there is going to be a trail of smaller positive or negative events leading up to it. Maybe throughout high school you were popular, a star athlete, and everything seemed to be going right for you. You were confident, brash, and could get almost anything you wanted (see? The laws of attraction were working).

Then you graduated, all of your friends went to work or school and you attended a local college because you couldn't get a scholarship to any of your prime choice universities. You weren't the star player on the team any longer and you began to lose confidence.

At the dorms, you made friends but there were quite a few people just like you and you didn't know how to cope not being the center of attention everywhere. Your attitude began to change. You changed.

Suddenly things started to fall apart for you. Tests were harder. You failed a class. You no longer had much interest in your declared major. You were benched from the team. You got into a fight for no reason.

And one day you sat alone in your car or dorm or out in the middle of the ball field wondering how things had turned sour so quickly. It was just a year or two earlier when life was great and you didn't have a care in the world.

A change occurred. It might have really been a minor one, but you focused on it and looked at it in a negative way. In time, you began to *think* negatively. You blamed the coach, the teacher, some other kids in the dorm, or even your parents.

The more negative or angry you became, the more bad things seemed to happen. It's a cycle and one that can get rougher and rougher if you don't know how to break out of it.

That's the *power of energy*. It will be drawn to the same forces, so when you begin to think negatively (such as, *I'm not going to get that job. There are too many other applicants and I just don't have anything to stand out about.*) then negative things are *more likely* to happen.

Thinking negatively doesn't always equal bad things happening, nor does thinking positively mean that positive things are going to occur all the time.

But the more you surround yourself with one form or another, the more that same energy is going to be drawn to you.

That's why, if you understand the laws of attraction and use them to your advantage, you can manifest wealth, love, happiness, and anything else that you can possibly want or imagine.

# Chapter 3 – Transforming Energy

As I noted in the previous chapter, the term 'transforming' is a bit of a misnomer. We can't actually transform energy polarity. We can transform energy and it happens every second of every day, but we can't transform positive energy into negative energy.

We can, however, transform the energy that *surrounds* us from one polarity to another and we don't need any fancy machines or devices to do it.

We simply need to rely on the power of our conscious mind.

**Know what you want.**

Most of us *think* we know what we want, but we actually don't. We might be chasing after what other people believe is best for us. We might be influenced by any number of creative and effective ads on TV or in magazines that make us believe if we *had* whatever they are selling, that we'd be happy.

It's simply not true. If you pay attention to any number of interviews with wealthy, downright rich people, a lot of them have similar emotional issues that we do. They aren't happy, they don't feel fulfilled, they're lonely ... it makes you wonder how that could possibly be, considering that they have all the money they'd ever need.

The truth is that they found out that money doesn't buy happiness. It can help you avoid stressing about your bills, but even extremely wealthy individuals find themselves in tremendous amounts of debt, just like the rest of us. For them, though, the fall can be farther and harder than what we might face.

You can also look at stories of people who won the lottery. They might have been working their whole lives and not getting anywhere and all they kept saying was, 'If we only had enough money to do this, that, or the other thing, we'd be happy.'

Then they play the right numbers and hit the big jackpot. They assume their troubles are over and life is going to be wonderful.

Yet that's not how it plays out.

The vast majority of these people end up flat broke, divorced, and miserable within 10 years. Those that win the huge jackpots ($100 million or more) are less likely to lose it all, but many of them end up having major problems as a result of the money.

Money doesn't solve problems. It usually only exacerbates them.

So if you're sitting there saying to yourself, 'If I only had more money, everything would be fine,' then you're not going to find abundance in your life (at least not the kind of abundance that adds value).

The first step is to *know what you want*.

Ask yourself what you truly want. Do you want people to adore you, to know who you are everywhere you go? You know, that can get tiring after a while. Once you have that, you will probably wish that you could just have some anonymity again.

Stephen King is one of the most successful novelists of our time and he is widely recognizable. His wife, Tabitha, is also an author and whenever she is out at a reading or book signing for one of her works and he shows up, she has to wonder whether people are there to see her, or him.

It's not all it's cracked up to be because when everyone knows you, it's hard to tell who likes you for you and who likes you *just* because you're popular, famous, or notorious.

What about a house? You want to own a house, right? But what kind of house? Where?

Do you want a 10,000 square foot mansion that you can get lost in? Who's going to clean it and maintain it? What would you do with all that space? Why would you even want something that big? For posterity? So the rest of the world could envy you?

Who cares?

If you live alone or have a family with two small children, three bedrooms is more than enough. Maybe four, if you want a home office.

What about location? Do you want to live on a lot of property so you can have privacy? Or maybe you prefer the city life. How about right near the ocean?

What about a job? Are you happy with your career choice? Does it fulfill you? Forget about the money factor at the moment. Do you enjoy your work? If not, then what did you always want to do or be when you were younger?

Often, the dreams of our youth are filled with stardust and daydreaming, but somewhere along the way you will have developed and affinity for some type of career that you may have forgotten about as you graduated high school and began to view opportunities based on resistance or money.

Go back to those youthful ambitions and see where your passions truly lie. You'll likely find what you would be happiest doing.

Now onto relationships. If you're married, you made a commitment to this other person. Unfortunately, too many people today jump into getting married because they *think* it's the right thing to do or they're afraid of losing their partner or for prestige. Divorce rates today exceed 50 percent. That means more than half of all marriages will end in divorce.

If you're not happy in this marriage or your current relationship, determine why. What are you *not* getting from it that you need? If it's sex, conversation, or other factors, these can potentially be improved, but you'd have to communicate them to your partner or spouse.

If you are simply not happy with the other person, the easy solution is to get a divorce or break it off, but you're going to have trouble in the next relationship as well. You need to determine what it is that you want and then build the positive forces around you. If you still aren't happy in this current relationship, then you'll need to end it in order to make room for a new one.

Cheating on your spouse or partner is negative and surrounds you with negativity. I find it interesting how so many people get involved with someone who is in a relationship or married, end up with that individual, and then are surprised years later when they cheat on *them*. You got involved with a cheater; they're not going to change. It's a negative relationship that will end up attracting negativity. Sure, you might be able to hide the negativity by buying a house together, making new friends, and having a honeymoon style period, but eventually the rose colored glasses will slip off and reality sinks in, which will be negative.

If you have difficulty determining what it is that you want, then you're going to be stuck in a negative loop. Knowing what you want helps to transform your force from negative into positive. Being realistic and not focused on impressing others will surround you with even more positive energy.

This is just the beginning. In the next chapter, we're going to help you figure out how to truly understand you and what you want, and what you deserve in life. Sometimes you need to step back, out of your own mind (in a manner of speaking) to be able to hear beyond the chaos and noise modern society throws our way.

Stepping out of negativity begins with small steps. Don't expect it to happen overnight. But like a snowball rolling down a steep hill, the process will begin to grow bigger, faster, and more powerful until you are nothing but a positive force in the world and attracting all sorts of abundance your way.

# Chapter 4 – Understanding *You*

How well do you know yourself?

Ask this question of the average teenager and you'll probably be met with a blank, glassy-eyed gaze. Ask a twenty-something and you'll be met with a confidence, almost arrogant attitude. Ask a thirty-something and you'll get a mix of answers.

Ask someone in their sixties or seventies and you're bound to find confidence without too much braggadocio. The older you get, the wiser you become. The wiser you become, the more you realize just what you don't know. In other words, when you're young, you *assume* that you know everything. When you get older, you realize how wrong you were and there's a transition period where you begin to discover your true inner desires and nature.

It's about understanding *you*. You may be young right now, or in your 40s or 50s or even older.

It's never too early or too late to begin figuring out who and what you are.

Understanding yourself is the first key to transforming the energy that surrounds you. When you are arrogant (don't confuse arrogance with confidence), you will be surrounding yourself with negative energy. Arrogance is brashness, over confidence without any real substance to back it up. Even if you're talented at something, being arrogant is drawing negativity to yourself.

Lebron James is a prime example of someone who was highly arrogant. Many would say that he had every right to be. He was highly touted for the NBA while he was still playing high school ball. Drafted into the pros right out of high school, he made an impact immediately.

His arrogance led to 'The Decision' to leave his home team, the Cleveland Cavaliers in such a fashion that he was scorned by many. It wasn't because he left, but *how* he left. His arrogance cost him many fans and would-be fans. He suddenly had so many people hating him and rooting against him that it was clearly bothering him during his first season with the Miami Heat.

He eventually won two championships and reached the finals all 4 years with the Miami Heat, but he also changed after that first season. He became a stronger leader for his team and tempered his arrogance and transformed it into confidence. When that happened, positive things began to happen for him.

So let's get involved and find out more about *you*.

### What you want.

We touched on this topic in the last chapter. But what do you want?

If you aren't quite sure, then how could you possibly expect to be able to attract *anything* to you?

"Well, I sort of want to have a family and a nice house somewhere, but I'm not sure where."

If you can't be concrete about what you want, if you don't have *confidence* to know exactly what you want, then you're throwing out a blurred concept to the universe.

What if you said you would like to, maybe, someday own a house, something decent and not too far away and then thirty years from now managed to purchase a home in a bad part of town where you never thought you'd live, but it's close to your job? Not exactly what you wanted, right?

Or was it? Let's look at that closer.

Someday you want to own a home. Thirty years from now is someday, right? So is 40 or 50 or even 60. Maybe you'd be upset if it takes you that long to buy something. You aren't specific.

Next, you wanted something 'decent.' What's 'dilapidated' to you might be decent or incredible to someone else. The universe doesn't know the difference. If you're not specific, you're leaving things open to wide interpretation.

'Not too far away' also leaves a lot of room open for interpretation. Not too far away from work? What's too far? 10 miles? 30? 100? Not too far from the ocean? Family? Your hometown?

You see, being tentative or indecisive is not going to provide you with a lot of positive energy. It's as though you don't feel like you could get what you *really* want, that you're not worthy, or that it will simply be out of your reach.

If you think like that, you're going to be thinking with *negativity*.

Stop it. Right now.

Be confident. Determine *what you want*.

If that's too challenging for you right now because there are so many things you'd be happy with, then start with what you *don't* want.

## What you don't want.

There are usually plenty of things you don't want. Debt. A bad relationship. Negative people. Jealous people. And so on.

Make a list of all of the things you really don't want in life. It could be an upper management position at a company. Or it could be working the line at the local diner.

No matter what it is, write it down. This will begin to highlight a pattern of what you don't really want.

You may begin seeing some of those very things surrounding you right now. If there are people who are in your life who bring you down, cause you aggravation, are too needy ... then it's time for you to consider cutting ties with them. This could be friends you've had for years, family members, or even your partner.

You don't need to break ties with them right now, but you need to identify the things that you don't want in your life.

## How to reach your true inner desires.

With so many ideas and thoughts floating around, all of the possibilities that life has to offer, it can feel overwhelming trying to determine what your true desires are any longer.

At some time in your past, you likely knew what those desires were. Then life began to become hectic. You found new responsibilities and were suddenly facing choices, like 'I have to take this job if I want to keep my apartment,' or 'I really want this new car even though it's going to be tough to afford, because I want people to see that I'm successful.'

All of this external noise gets in the way of your *true* desires.

In order to shake off all of that noise, you need to get yourself to a quiet place. This could be your own home if you live alone, or a particular room in it if you don't. Turn off all of the distractions and make sure everyone knows that you need to be undisturbed for a period of time.

Once you get to that quiet place, begin to reflect on your life, from your teenage years to right now. Think about all of the things that you *thought* you would want to become, or jobs that you wanted to do.

Write them down.

Next, remember what you saw as an ideal relationship when you were younger, when talking to someone of the opposite sex was a downright nerve-racking prospect for you. What was most important to you then?

Was it their looks? Was it their smile? Was it the way that they were kind to other people, especially those who were picked on? Was it because they were responsible?

What do you go after now? Are you chasing the 'hot' looking girl or guy? Are you chasing someone who seems 'dangerous' or 'bad'?

Why do you do that? Is it because you're seeking adventure? You want to change someone else? Too many people get into bad relationships because they believe they'll change the other person. In truth, they're the ones that need to change but they can't face that, so they go after people they see as 'broken.' Then, when it becomes clear they can't change the other person, the relationship turns sour.

Write down what *is* really most important to you with a relationship.

Then begin to focus on your living situation. What kind of home would you be most comfortable in? Would it be a house in a rural setting? Near water such as a lake, river, or the ocean? Have you always wanted to live in another part of the country? Why?

How many bedrooms will you need? What kind of neighbors do you want?

The more details that you can write down now, the more specific you'll be. The more specific you are, the more positive the energy surrounding you will become.

## Why knowing all of this is important.

In order to attract the things you want to you, you need to have a clear idea about what it is you specifically want. If you're unclear about things, then the energy you surround yourself will tend to be negative.

Also, if you're not clear on what you want, then when you *do* get certain things, you might not be happy with them for long.

You need to find a way to get past the clutter in your life that comes in the form of confusion. The clearer you are, the more easily you'll be able to attract abundance into your life.

You'll then begin to discover so many other wonderful things happening to and around you that you'll wonder how you ever managed to survive before.

And that, my friends, is a *wonderful* feeling. I can testify to that!

## Chapter 5 – Attract the Things You Want

Once you have a good understanding about *what* you want, you then need to focus on ways to go out and get them. A lot of people rely on different strategies in the pursuit of the things they want.

Some are successful. Others are not quite as successful. Still others fail.

In fact, the vast majority of people fail in the pursuit of their goals.

Keep in mind this one fundamental thing: *nothing* is out of your reach. Not a single thing. Yes, there are limitations and stipulations to this, though. If you stand 5 feet, 6 inches tall, you're not going to play in the NBA. You're also not likely to make it onto any professional sports team where the average player is well over six feet tall.

If you're in your 30s, you're not likely to fly into outer space, *unless you manage to earn tens of millions of dollars and can buy a ticket.*

However, we're not talking about wild dreams here; we're talking about realistic and very achievable goals.

You want to be wealthy so that you don't need to worry about how much you'll have left over after your next paycheck.

Fine.

You want to be filled with happiness.

Good (but *no one* is happy *all the time*).

You want a rewarding career.

No problem.

You want to be successful.

That all depends on your definition of success. If it's reasonable (in reference to what I just mentioned), then it's certainly possible.

You want good health.

Great.

You want abundance in life. All of these things that we've mentioned, just more of it.

Take it.

The key is learning how to achieve these things. Let's explore them each together.

## Wealth

Most people have a desire to have money. So what is wealth?

Wealth is basically defined as having enough money to enjoy the luxuries in life. This could be a vacation house, a fancy car (aside from your main vehicle), a nice boat, wonderful clothes, an expansive house with all the best furnishings, and more.

You need to define wealth for yourself. How much money do you believe would be enough for you? If you're living on $20,000 a year right now, $100,000 could seem like true wealth. If you're earning $100,000 a year, and you're still struggling to make ends meet, then you might define wealth differently.

Wealth is really not about *money*, but the amount of money you earn on a regular and consistent basis coupled with the assets that you acquire over time. Your assets would be cars, houses, possessions, and such.

In order to attract wealth to you, it's necessary for you to have a clear understanding of what wealth is *to you*. Does this mean that *when* you are finally wealthy that you won't change your mind and decide that you want more? No. You could certainly end up in that situation.

But you need to begin with a clear understanding about how *you* define wealth. Let's say you are renting an apartment and have a job that pays you $10 per hour. That's approximately $22,000 per year.

You want to earn $100,000 per year and own a home. Set that as your goal and give yourself a reasonable amount of time to achieve it. If you think that you're going to be wealthy like that in 1 year, you're going to be disappointed and that's going to lead to negativity, which is going to repel wealth once again.

## Happiness

You're tired of being unhappy. But you're not sure why. If you can't define happiness for yourself, then how can you expect to be happy?

This is one of the major stumbling blocks for people who claim to want to be happy and they're not: they simply don't know what will make them happy. If you don't know, then you're drawing negative energy to you.

If you know what is going to make you happy, then you're going to be able to think positively and *then* attract happiness to you.

Determine what will make you happy. Avoid assuming that material possessions, such as a sports car, diamond necklaces, or even a 70-inch flat screen TV is going to bring you happiness. Marketers make you *think* that's the case, but it will only appear to fill a void for a brief amount of time.

## Love

You want to be in love. You want to find someone who will make you happy, cause your heart to skip a beat whenever you see her or him, and who will challenge you to be a better person.

So are you going to find this in a person whose only positive attribute is their looks? Probably not. That's a superficial aspect that will fulfill shallow or insecure people, not someone with depth of thought or who wants more out of life and fleeting appearances.

Remember, eventually everyone will age and those 'hot' looks will fade and you'll be left with someone with whom you'll need to be happy with on other accounts.

Be clear on what is *most* important to you in a relationship. If it's their appearance, then that is going to draw negative energy to you. If appearance is just one aspect of what you want in your partner, then you will be drawing positivity to you because the universe understands that there's more than meets the eye when it comes to attraction.

**Career**

You may have a job, but do you have a *career?* A career is the overall field in which we work. If you work at a restaurant and you enjoy cooking, then you might have a career in the food industry. If you enjoy building and designing things, you might prefer a career in architecture.

Hemming and hawing about what you want to do, like far too many young people do today, is not going to provide you with the right opportunities.

Being clear and focused will bring positive energy your way.

## Success

Like wealth, success is defined different for various people. You may find that playing music on the weekends with your band will be a success. You don't need to 'make it big' or be selling thousands of CDs every month.

The clearer you are about success and what it would be for you, the more you will attract success to you.

Success may involve your wealth, your relationships, your career, health, the things you will still be able to do into your 60s or 70s, and much more.

Focus on determining what will define success for you with *all* of those things.

## Health

You could be a physical specimen of ultimate health and fitness right now and you probably want to maintain that as long as possible. Yet when you begin to worry about every little cough, sniffle, pain, wart, or growth on your body, you begin to surround yourself with negativity and then you will likely begin to get sick.

Focus on ways that you can stay healthy and when something changes on or in your body, don't stress about it too much.

This doesn't mean you won't have to worry about cancer or other health problems. But the more *positive* you are about your heath, the healthier you will become.

And when you do face a health crisis, when you have a habit of being healthy, it's going to have a direct impact on how well you overcome this new challenge.

## Abundance

People who struggle to get things in life are spending most of their time stressed and worrying about what they are going to have next year or month or week.

Abundance in today's society (within the past couple of years) is being frowned upon. If you're successful, if you have 'too much' or more than other people have, you're going to be vilified.

Forget those naysayers. The truth is that those who don't have either don't understand the laws of attraction or don't make the effort to get those things.

There is *nothing wrong with abundance.* If you want an abundance of wealth, happiness, love, success, health, or anything else, go and get it.

The only thing stopping you is you.

And the energy with which you surround yourself.

In order to be able to attract the things you want, you need to have a clear picture of what *exactly* it is that you want. Once you have that, you will begin to naturally draw more positive energy your way.

It's that positive flow of energy that will bring all of the things you want closer to you.

Now you just need to learn how to ask for the things you want.

# Chapter 6 – Learning to Ask for the Things You Want

In order for you to get the things that you want, you need to learn how to ask for them. It's not like asking for a raise or asking your parents to borrow the car for the weekend.

Asking in this sense is asking the universe. And it's about surrounding yourself with the right energy.

If you want a better job and you have figured out exactly what you want, then you need to surround yourself with the positive belief that it *will* happen.

But that's not enough. You still need to go out and do the things necessary to get them done. For example, if you want to change your career, you may need to go back to college. You need to put in the effort to learn more about your new goals.

But if you sit there and think that you're too old, that it will cost too much, or it will take too much time, or you won't do well enough in college courses, then you'll never achieve it.

It all starts with the initial force of energy that you envelope yourself in. You need to be able to open yourself up to what you want.

## Law of attraction begins by opening yourself up to what you want.

The law of attraction begins by opening yourself up to the things you want. When you are at a party and you don't know anyone, what do you do?

If you're like a lot of people who struggle with their self confidence and image, you might tend to slink over to a corner of the room to watch and observe. Your shoulders hunch over and you fold over in on yourself. At least, that's how other people will view you (that's the impression you'll give off).

You're not attracting anyone. You will then likely go home alone without having met anyone new, unless people seek you out.

When it comes to these things that you want, if you are closed to them, if you don't believe that they can come true or come to you, then you're essentially drawing nothing but negativity to you and that will attract the bad things, which is what you might already be expecting.

You attract what you put out there.

Begin opening yourself up to new possibilities. Begin to believe that *you are worthy* of these things. It takes practice. Things are not going to go your way every time, and if you slip back into old habits of believing that you can't, you won't, you're not worthy ... then you repel the things you want deep down.

Start your day off by resetting yourself.

It doesn't matter what happened the day before. You could have been late to work. You could have been stuck in traffic. Your car could have broken down. You might have broken your ankle tripping down the stairs rushing out the door.

It could have been the absolute worst day of your life, but that next morning you get an opportunity to completely reset the meter.

Every day is a new day.

It may be a platitude, but it's also an *attitude*.

Every day is a new day with new opportunities to grab onto.

Forget the bad things that happened the day before. Remind yourself that converting from surrounding yourself in negative energy to positive energy is a process. **It's going to take time!**

You will fail many times before you succeed.

Michael Jordan, arguably the greatest basketball player in the history of the game, starred in a famous Nike commercial from the mid-1990s, during the peak of his championship successes. In that commercial, he talked about the thousands of shots he missed, the hundreds of games he lost, and the dozens of times he was entrusted with the game winning shot ... and missed. It closed by him saying ...

"I have failed over and over again in my life ... and that is why I succeed."

You need to stop being afraid of failing. Every failure is going to bring you closer to your success.

If you shy away from it or get down about those failures, then you're going to be drawing negative energy to you, which will then collectively bring more negativity to your life.

So every morning, open yourself up to success.

Stand up out of bed, stretch, roll your head along your neck, then look in the mirror and say, "Today I will get everything I want. Today is going to be a *great* day. This is *my* day."

When you begin to make yourself more attractive to positive things, you will find that they begin to come to you more and more and more.

But it's a process. You can't just wake up one morning, say this, and then have everything work out for you. It will take time, patience, and consistency. Shaking off the negative energy is tough. It's the negative energy that tends to be attracted to us by default, especially if you've been surrounding yourself with it for all these years.

**Asking is important.**

You also need to learn to ask for the things you want. It's not enough to simply state that you would like a bigger house or nicer clothing or a better relationship. You need to ask for those things of the universe.

A person who stands in the middle of a square or a courtyard or even a busy city intersection is probably not going to get what he or she wants. After all, with the thousands upon thousands of people who will walk past him during the day, will even a single one have the first clue what he wants unless he lets them know?

No.

The universe isn't going to know, either. You need to put your requests out there.

I would like to build a new career doing architecture.

I want to have a relationship I can be happy with.

I want to own a house in two years.

I want to be living in California (or Florida, New York, France, or wherever you want).

Whatever you want in life, you need to make sure that you ask for those things. It's not that the universe is just going to bring them to you, but it's more an affirmation that you really do want them.

Get in the habit of asking for these things on a daily basis. Whatever it is that you want, ask for it. Just be prepared to accept it when it happens.

## Open yourself up to allow these things into your life.

I mentioned that you're going to have to open yourself up to positive energy in order to get the things that you truly want. You're also going to need to open yourself up and *accept* them when they come to you.

Maybe you want the intelligent, attractive woman who would rate a '10' on most attractive scales. She's been way 'out of your league' for your entire life, but you want that woman.

Maybe you had your eye on a specific woman, but she could be married. You're not going to expect to win her over and away from her husband. That would be surrounded by negative energy. Even if you were able to succeed, it would be tainted by negative energy and other things would most likely begin to go wrong for you.

We already talked about the problems going after a married person, anyway.

So let's say that you want an attractive, intelligent person to fall for you. Once you begin to develop a positive attitude and outlook on life, you're going to notice that people are attracted to you.

Suddenly you find yourself talking to the woman of your dreams and things are going great. You exchange phone numbers and you're all excited to call and ask her out on a date.

But you stop yourself. Every time you pick up the phone, the old you is coming back into focus. It's that voice in your head telling you that she's out of your league, that you don't really stand a chance with her, that she's just trying to get something out of you.

You begin to close yourself off. You begin to revert to what's most comfortable to you ... being negative.

For the vast majority of people, being negative is the default ideology. They can't find a way to be positive. They don't really want to. It's easier to believe that you deserve your lot in life, that it's too difficult to achieve your dreams or goals.

Being positive and attracting the best things to us is very, very difficult.

When you begin to become more positive, *things will be drawn to you.* You need to be ready and willing to accept them when they do.

Too many people have a guilt complex when things start working out the way they always wanted. You might feel that you don't deserve it, or you see someone else who is struggling or bad things are happening to them. So you step back and think, 'Do I really deserve all of these good, positive things when so many other people are suffering?'

Why not?

Don't buy into this socialist ideology that we are all supposed to have the same things, have the same amount of money, have the same opportunities. That only leads to one place ... misery for *everyone*.

We are responsible for our ultimate successes and failures. Some people will work harder than others. Some people will believe in the laws of attraction and will naturally lure the best of things *to* them.

In this country, the United States, *everyone* is given opportunity. What you do with it is up to you. When success comes to you, whether through hard work, a positive attitude, perseverance, or just plain luck, you don't need to feel guilty about it. Use your success to actually make a difference in others' lives. Don't shut it off or shut out those wonderful blessings because you feel guilty.

Be willing to accept them when they happen.

*Afraid of success.*

We've often heard about people who are afraid of failure, but what about being afraid of success? That's actually more common among many people, and it's why so many people get so far in life and then no further. They are afraid to be successful.

A writer who studies his entire life and writes book after book after book, *knowing* that he's a great writer, may never submit his work because deep down he's afraid of being successful.

Once you find success, you might begin to worry that next time will be a failure, or that you'll be exposed to more skilled people who might see you as a fraud.

Get past it. Keep embracing the positives in life. Manifest abundance in your life by being positive, by eliminating the negatives in life, and by focusing on being specific about *what you want*.

When you do, you'll attract everything you want, no matter what it might be. Money, the ideal partner, the dream home … *anything*.

Just be ready for it and willing to accept it. Otherwise you could very easily see it all slip back through your proverbial fingers.

# Chapter 7 – Real Stories of People Who Used the Laws of Attraction

Nothing drives a point home better than actual stories of people who did what you have only dreamed of to this point in your life.

The following stories are real. They are of real people who had, at one time in their life or another, felt as though nothing good would ever happen to or for them. You'll probably be able to relate to at least a couple of them.

*Mandy Simmons*

Mandy was 38 years old and newly divorced. It was a bitter divorce and a big part of her was grateful that they didn't have children together. She wanted kids, but by the time she realized what her husband was truly like, she didn't want to have any with him.

She was devastated by the divorce. She lost most of the friends she had made during her five year marriage (they all stayed friends with him and bought into his lies about her, mostly because he had money and was confident). She didn't know what she was going to do.

She moped around for about a year until her best friend told her it was time to 'snap out of it.'

So she did. She learned about the laws of attraction and was able to look back on the past ten years of her life and see how negative she had been. She was attractive, but she gave up on a career because she wanted a husband and children. She wanted a successful husband who had money and good looks. She met Tom and the rest was history.

She was never really happy, though. Now she wanted something else. She wanted a career. She was a great cook and had thought about building a catering company. She wasn't interested in a relationship again, but if she did meet the right guy, someone who was kind and patient and had a fairly decent job, she wouldn't turn him away.

She just didn't need all the baggage that had come with her past relationships.

Every morning Mandy woke up and recited her affirmations, that she was worthy, that she was smart, that she could do anything she wanted.

She got a job working for a caterer, squirreled away her money while learning all about the business from the inside. She didn't mind the long hours, the weekends lost, or any of those things she thought were so important.

Within three years, she started her own company and it took off. She was soon hiring a dozen people to work for her, bought a few vans, and met a man at a wedding she catered.

Soon she had everything she wanted and it was all because of the laws of attraction.


*Bryan Reynolds*

A young go-getter, Bryan had often impressed his bosses with his willingness to work late, run errands, and do whatever they wanted of him. They knew he'd be climbing that corporate ladder.

But Bryan was only doing it for one reason: money.

He wanted to earn more and more money. The more he made, the more he spent; usually on more expensive clothes, a nice car, and things to impress 'the ladies.'

By the time he was 30, he was closing in on a senior executive position, but he was lonely. He wasn't happy. Nothing he bought mattered to him any longer. He soon found that his job was a burden, but he was going to continue doing it because that's what made the most sense.

He heard about the laws of attraction and decided to focus on it. He determined that he didn't want to be a corporate executive forever; he wanted his own business. He wanted to get out of the rat race. He had always loved vacationing down at the Florida Keys and thought about how cool it would be to open a bar up along the beaches there.

He began to focus on positivity and being clear about the things he wanted. Within 5 years, he was serving margaritas on the beach from his own bar and life couldn't be better.

The more positive things came to him, the more successful his life became.

*Tom Forsythe*

By the time Tom was 56, he had raised three children, was widowed, and felt that the best years of his life were now tucked behind him. He was battling depression and financial hardships. His company of 32 years had laid him off and while he had a pension, it was a fraction of what he had expected it to be.

His children were all busy doing their own thing and didn't have time for him.

Tom was in a bookstore one afternoon and noticed a book about attracting the things you always wanted to you. He was intrigued, so he bought it on a whim.

By the time he finished reading, he was both skeptical, but excited. He realized that skepticism was just negativity dressed up in a fancy suit. So he shook that off right away.

Then he began to focus on letting other negative thoughts go, chasing them away when he recognized them sneaking in.

Tom then thought long and hard about what he wanted for the next 20 years of his life. He wanted to live down south somewhere. South Carolina, he thought. Maybe Florida.

He wanted to learn to play golf, scuba dive, and meet new friends. His old self would have told him a hundred reasons why this wasn't practical, but as he developed a new positive attitude, things began to work out just right to bring him those things.

He received an ad in the mail for property in South Carolina. He couldn't believe it. He hadn't even looked into that prospect yet, but there it was, in his mailbox.

He ended up buying a condo in a retirement community that had a golf course. He bought clubs and learned.

He was growing happier by the day and making some wonderful friends. He even met a single woman whom he ended up marrying two years later.

Once the positive things started coming into his life, more came along as well.

What is your story going to say? Are you going to embrace the fact that energy begets energy, that positive energy attracts positive energy and that negative energy attracts negative energy?

Or are you going to close this book and ignore the laws of attraction. You read this for a reason: you are unfulfilled at the moment. It's time to get fulfilled again.

The laws of attraction are real. They work. And they *will* bring you abundance if you let them.

# **Conclusion**

No matter where you live, the laws of attraction will work for you. The key is to believe in them.

This isn't about some magic trick or some snake oil that isn't going to actually do anything for you. This is real.

Changing your life is as simple (and complicated) as making a choice. It's complicated because actually *doing* something differently than you've been doing your whole life is going to take effort and persistence. It's simple because *all you need to do is tell yourself that you want to do it*.

Being positive when you're feeling like something someone dragged in on the bottom of your shoes is not easy. But it's possible.

Start off your day with affirmations that you're worthy, that you're smart, that *you can do this*, and keep repeating them until you truly do believe it.

Whenever you find yourself slipping throughout the day, repeat your positive affirmations. Positive energy comes from the notion, so eventually you'll begin to feel the **pull** of that change in your life.

And it will feel great.

Nothing is out of reach, as long as you believe it's possible. If you don't believe it's possible, then why should the universe accommodate you.

So what are you waiting for? Be positive.

You're worth it.

## Other books available by author on Kindle, Paperback and Audio

Creative Visualization and Self Hypnosis: How to Use the Power of Your Imagination and Self Hypnosis to Create What You Want in Life

Made in the USA
Las Vegas, NV
06 May 2022